Chapter 3: Advanced Feed Recipes

- Organic Chicken Feed
- Non-GMO Chicken Feed
- Soy-Free and Corn-Free Feed Recipes
- Grower Feeds
- Layer Feeds
- Broiler Feeds

Chapter 4: Feeding Strategies

- Free-Range Feeding
- Feeding for Optimal Health
- Feeding for Egg Production
- Feeding for Meat Production

Chapter 5: Supplementing Feed

- Kitchen Scraps
- Greens and Herbs
- Protein Supplements
- Mineral Supplements

Chapter 6: Troubleshooting and FAQ

- Common Feeding Problems
- Frequently Asked Questions
- Tips for Making Homemade Feed

Conclusion

- The Advantages of Homemade Chicken Feed
- Next Steps for Implementing Homemade Feed
- Additional Resources

Introduction

Raising chickens can be a rewarding and enjoyable experience, but
one of the most important aspects of keeping chickens is providing

Homemade Chicken Feed: A Complete Guide and Recipe Book for Your Flock

As a consumer who raises chickens, I am always on the lookout for ways to save money on feed while also ensuring that my birds are getting the best possible nutrition. In recent years, feed prices have risen dramatically and there have been shortages of certain ingredients, making it more challenging than ever to find affordable, high-quality feed options. Additionally, I am concerned about the ingredients that are used in commercial chicken feeds and want to make sure that I am providing my birds with a diet that is free from harmful additives and fillers.

To address these concerns, I have begun experimenting with homemade chicken feed recipes. By making my own feed, I am able to control the ingredients and ensure that my birds are getting a diet that is tailored to their specific needs. Additionally, making my own feed allows me to save money on feed costs and avoid the unpredictability of the commercial feed market.

In this book, I will share with you some of my favorite homemade chicken feed recipes that are affordable, easy to make, and full of nutritious ingredients. Whether you are a seasoned chicken keeper or a newbie just getting started, you will find plenty of ideas and inspiration for creating a healthy, sustainable diet for your birds.

Happy Farming!

Table of Contents

Introduction

them with a balanced and nutritious diet. In recent years, feed prices have risen dramatically and there have been shortages of certain ingredients, making it more challenging than ever to find affordable, high-quality feed options. Additionally, many commercial chicken feeds contain harmful additives and fillers that can have negative effects on the health and well-being of your birds.

Making your own chicken feed at home is an excellent solution to these problems. It allows you to control the ingredients and ensure that your birds are getting a diet that is tailored to their specific needs. Additionally, making your own feed can save you money on feed costs and avoid the unpredictability of the commercial feed market.

The Ultimate Guide to Homemade Chicken Feed is a strategic guide that will teach you everything you need to know about making your own chicken feed. From understanding the nutritional needs of chickens to learning how to make different types of feed, this book covers it all. You'll learn about the benefits of homemade feed, the various feed ingredients and their nutritional value, and how to create a balanced and nutritious diet for your birds.

The recipes provided in this book are easy to make and use affordable, readily available ingredients. You'll find recipes for basic feed, advanced feed, and feed for specific purposes such as growing, laying, and meat production. The book also covers feeding strategies, supplementing feed, troubleshooting common problems and answers frequently asked questions.

This guide is perfect for both new and experienced chicken keepers who are looking for ways to improve the health and well-being of their birds while also saving money on feed costs. Whether you're raising chickens for eggs or meat, this guide will provide you with all the information and resources you need to create a healthy and sustainable diet for your birds.

Chapter 1: Understanding Chicken Nutrition

Understanding the nutritional needs of chickens is essential for providing them with a balanced and nutritious diet. Chickens require a variety of nutrients to stay healthy, including protein, carbohydrates, fat, vitamins, and minerals. In this chapter, we will take a closer look at the specific nutritional requirements of chickens and the different feed ingredients that can be used to meet those needs.

Protein is a vital nutrient for chickens and plays an important role in their growth, feather development, and egg production. Chickens require a minimum of 18% protein in their diet to meet their nutritional needs.

Soybean meal is a common protein source in chicken feed, as it is high in protein and contains all the essential amino acids that chickens need. It is also an affordable and readily available ingredient. Fish meal is another protein source that is high in protein and omega-3 fatty acids, which are beneficial for chickens' health. However, it is important to note that fish meal can be expensive and may not be readily available in some areas.

Meat and bone meal is another protein source that is often used in chicken feed. It is made from rendered animal parts, such as bones, blood, and offal, and is an excellent source of protein, as well as calcium, phosphorus, and other minerals. However, it is important to be aware that some types of meat and bone meal may contain harmful additives, such as antibiotics and hormones, and should be avoided.

It is also important to note that not all protein sources are created equal, and chickens may require different types of protein at different stages of their life. For example, during the growth phase, chickens require a diet that is higher in protein to support their rapid growth, while during the laying phase, a diet with moderate protein levels is more suitable.

In addition, some chicken breeds may require a different balance of protein sources to meet their nutritional needs. For example, heritage breeds may require a higher protein diet than commercial breeds.

Therefore, it is important to consider the specific nutritional needs of your chickens and the protein sources that are available to you when creating homemade chicken feed. By providing your birds with a diet that meets their specific nutritional needs, you can ensure that they are healthy, happy, and productive.

Mealworms can be fed to chickens as a supplement to their regular feed, or as a treat. They can be fed live or dried, and can be stored for long periods of time. Dried mealworms can be stored in an airtight container in a cool, dry place, and can be rehydrated before feeding.

When feeding mealworms to chickens, it is important to provide them in moderation, as they are high in fat and too much can lead to obesity in chickens. Additionally, it's important to note that some chickens may be allergic to mealworms and should avoid them.

Mealworms can be a great supplement to the chickens' diet, they are a good source of protein and other nutrients. They can also be a great source of entertainment for chickens, as they love to hunt and forage for them.

In addition, using mealworms as a protein source in chicken feed can be an environmentally friendly and sustainable alternative to traditional protein sources such as soy or fish meal. They have a relatively low environmental impact, and are easy to produce and harvest. My guide for mealworm farming can be found here. https://bit.ly/MealWormBook

Carbohydrates are an important energy source for chickens and are found in various grains such as corn, wheat, and barley. They provide chickens with the energy they need to perform daily activities and maintain a healthy body weight. Chickens require a minimum of 2% carbohydrates in their diet to meet their nutritional needs.

Corn is a common carbohydrate source in chicken feed, as it is high in energy and easily digestible. It is also a good source of vitamins and minerals, such as vitamin A, B12, and E, as well as minerals like potassium, zinc, and iron. However, it's important to note that corn is a common allergen and may not be suitable for all chickens.

Wheat is another carbohydrate source that is often used in chicken feed. It is high in energy and provides chickens with a good source of carbohydrates, as well as vitamins and minerals, such as vitamin B6, B12, and E, along with minerals like iron, zinc, and copper.

Barley is another carbohydrate source that is often used in chicken feed. It is a good source of energy and provides chickens with a good source of carbohydrates, as well as vitamins and minerals, such as vitamin B6, B12, and E, along with minerals like iron, zinc, and copper.

It is important to note that chickens have different nutritional requirements at different stages of their life. For example, young chickens, or chicks, require a higher carbohydrate content in their diet than adult chickens to support their rapid growth. We will cover this in chapters ahead. Similarly, chickens that are being raised for meat production will have different carbohydrate requirements than those being raised for egg production.

Additionally, the environment in which chickens are kept can also affect their carbohydrate needs. For example, chickens that are free-range and have access to grass and insects will have different carbohydrate needs than those that are kept in confinement.

One other thing to consider when using carbohydrates as a source of energy for chickens is the form in which they are fed. Whole grains such as corn, wheat, and barley are more difficult for chickens to digest than ground or cracked grains. Chickens have a relatively short digestive tract, so they are not able to digest whole grains as easily as they can ground or cracked grains. So when using these grains, it is important to grind or crack them first to make them more easily digestible for the chickens.

Also, the quality of the grains. It is important to use high-quality grains that are free from mold, moisture, and other contaminants, as these can be harmful to chickens.

Take in to consideration the type of feeder you use to feed the chickens. Feeders are an important aspect of providing chickens with a balanced diet. The type of feeder you use can affect the amount of feed available to the chickens and help prevent overeating, which can lead to obesity and other health issues.

There are several types of feeders that can be used for chickens, each with their own advantages and disadvantages. Some of the most common types of feeders include:

- Trough feeders: These are the most traditional type of feeders and are typically made of wood or plastic. They are long and narrow and are placed on the ground or on a raised platform. Trough feeders are easy to fill and clean, but they can be difficult to regulate the amount of feed available to the chickens.
- Hanging feeders: These feeders are suspended from the ceiling or from a wall-mounted bracket. They are typically

made of metal or plastic and have a lid that can be opened for filling and cleaning. Hanging feeders are easy to use and are great for preventing chickens from scratching feed out of the feeder and wasting it.

- Automatic feeders: These feeders are powered by electricity or batteries and can be programmed to dispense feed at specific intervals. They are typically made of metal or plastic and are great for preventing overeating and ensuring that chickens have access to feed at all times.
- Self-feeders: These feeders are designed to be refilled by the chickens as they eat. They are typically made of metal or plastic and have a hopper that is filled with feed. The chickens can access the feed through a dispenser at the bottom of the hopper. These feeders are great for preventing waste, but they can be more expensive than other types of feeders.

It's also important to note that different chicken breeds have different nutritional requirements and that chickens have different nutritional requirements at different stages of their life. Additionally, the environment in which chickens are kept can also affect their nutritional needs. So it's a good idea to consult with a veterinarian or poultry nutritionist to ensure that the feeder you are using meets the specific nutritional needs of your chickens.

Keep in mind that chickens have different nutritional requirements at different stages of their life. For example, young chickens, or chicks, require a higher carbohydrate content in their diet than adult chickens to support their rapid growth. Similarly, chickens that are being raised for meat production will have different carbohydrate requirements than those being raised for egg production.

Overall, carbohydrates are an important energy source for chickens, but it's important to consider the form in which they are fed, the quality of the grains, the type of feeder used, and the nutritional needs of your chickens when creating a homemade chicken feed recipe. By providing your birds with a diet that meets their specific nutritional needs, you can ensure that they are healthy, happy, and productive.

Fat is an important macronutrient for chickens, as it provides them with energy, helps to keep their skin and feathers healthy, and aids in the absorption of certain vitamins and minerals. Chickens require a fat content of at least 2% in their diet.

Common sources of fat in chicken feed include vegetable oil, such as corn oil, soybean oil, or canola oil, and animal fat, such as chicken fat or fish oil. These fats provide chickens with a balanced source of energy and help to keep them warm in cold weather.

Vegetable oils are a great source of fat for chickens because they are rich in essential fatty acids, such as linoleic acid and linolenic acid, which are important for maintaining healthy skin and feathers. Animal fats, on the other hand, are a great source of energy for chickens, as they are more calorie-dense than vegetable oils.

It's important to note that not all fats are created equal, and it's important to provide chickens with a balanced source of fats. For example, vegetable oils are high in polyunsaturated fats, which are more easily oxidized and can become rancid, whereas animal fats are high in saturated fats, which are more stable and have a longer shelf life.

It's also important to note that chickens have different fat requirements depending on their environment, life stage, and breed. For example, chickens that are kept in a confined environment or that are being raised for egg production will require a higher fat content in their diet than chickens that are allowed to forage for food or that are being raised for meat production.

It's a good idea to consult with a veterinarian or poultry nutritionist to ensure that the feed recipe you are using meets the specific fat requirements of your chickens. By providing your chickens with a diet that is rich in the right types of fats, you can ensure that they are healthy, happy, and productive.

Vitamins and minerals are essential micronutrients that play a crucial role in maintaining overall health and well-being in chickens. These micronutrients are required in small amounts, but they play a vital role in various bodily functions such as growth, reproduction, and immune function. Some common vitamins and minerals found in chicken feed include Vitamin A, Vitamin D, Vitamin E, calcium, and phosphorus.

Vitamin A is important for maintaining good vision, healthy skin, and a strong immune system. Vitamin D is necessary for the absorption of calcium and phosphorus, which are important for bone growth and development. Vitamin E is an antioxidant that helps to protect cells from damage and supports the immune system.

Calcium and phosphorus are important minerals for chickens, as they are necessary for proper bone growth and development. Chickens that do not receive enough calcium and phosphorus in their diet may develop weak bones or suffer from other health problems.

You should note that chickens have different vitamin and mineral requirements depending on their environment, life stage, and breed. For example, chickens that are kept in a confined environment or that are being raised for egg production will require more calcium in their diet than chickens that are allowed to forage for food or that are being raised for meat production. Similarly, chickens in different stage of life have different requirements, for example, chicks require more vitamins and minerals than adult chickens.

Water is an essential component of a chicken's diet, as it is necessary for maintaining overall health and well-being. Chickens require a source of water to stay hydrated and support various bodily functions such as digestion, metabolism, and thermoregulation.

It's important to provide chickens with clean, fresh water at all times. This means that their water source should be free of debris, algae, and bacteria. Chickens should have access to water at all times, as they will drink water throughout the day and night. The water should be kept at a moderate temperature that is comfortable for the chickens, not too cold or too hot.

Chickens will drink more water in hot weather, so it's important to monitor the water levels in their feeders during the summer months, and refill them as necessary. Chickens will also drink more water if they are eating a diet that is high in protein or if they are producing more eggs.

It's a good idea to have multiple water sources available to your chickens, so that they can choose where to drink from. For example, if you have a large flock, you might want to provide a water source for each group or section of chickens.

In addition, it's important to regularly clean and sanitize the chicken's waterers to prevent the build-up of bacteria and parasites. This can be done by cleaning the waterers with hot, soapy water and then rinsing them thoroughly.

By providing your chickens with clean, fresh water at all times, you can ensure that they are hydrated and healthy. This is crucial for the overall well-being of your chickens, and will help to ensure that they are productive and able to resist illness.

When creating homemade chicken feed, it is important to use a variety of ingredients to ensure that your birds are getting all the nutrients they need. Some common feed ingredients include whole grains, such as corn and wheat, as well as legumes such as soybeans, peas, and lentils. Additionally, a variety of kitchen scraps can be used to supplement chicken feed, such as vegetables, fruits, and even coffee grounds.

When making your own chicken feed, it is important to use high-quality ingredients that are free from harmful additives. Organic and non-GMO ingredients are best, as they are free from pesticides, herbicides, and genetically modified organisms. If you're looking for a soy-free and corn-free feed, you can use alternative ingredients like oats, barley, and millet.

However, there are also other factors to consider when it comes to chicken nutrition. For example, chickens have different nutritional requirements at different stages of their life. Young chickens, or chicks, require a higher protein content in their diet than adult chickens. Similarly, chickens that are being raised for meat production will have different nutritional requirements than those being raised for egg production.

Additionally, the environment in which chickens are kept can also affect their nutritional needs. For example, chickens that are free-range and have access to grass and insects will have different nutritional needs than those that are kept in confinement.

In later chapters, we will delve deeper into these topics and discuss how to create feed recipes and feeding strategies that are tailored to the specific needs of your chickens. We will also cover additional ways to supplement chicken feed, such as through kitchen scraps, greens and herbs, and mineral and protein supplements.

So, we have covered the basic nutritional needs of chickens, including protein, carbohydrates, fat, vitamins and minerals, and water. We have also discussed the importance of using high-quality ingredients and understanding feed labels and ingredients when making your own chicken feed.

Now we will discuss the different feeding needs of chickens at different life stages. Chickens have different nutritional requirements at different stages of their life, and it's important to understand these needs in order to provide them with the proper nutrition.

Starting with the first stage, the chick stage, newly hatched chicks require a high-protein diet to support their rapid growth and development. When making your own feed, it's important to include ingredients that are high in protein to meet the needs of your chicks. Some good options include soybean meal, fish meal, and meat and bone meal. Additionally, make sure to add in essential vitamins and minerals such as Vitamin A, Vitamin D, Vitamin E, calcium, and phosphorus to support the growth and development of your chicks. It's recommended to feed this high protein diet for the first 6-8 weeks of their life.

The exact ratio of protein to other ingredients in your homemade chick starter feed will depend on the specific ingredients you choose to use. However, as a general guideline, a good starting point is to aim for a protein content of around 20-22%. This can be achieved by using protein-rich ingredients such as soybean meal, fish meal, or meat and bone meal, and combining them with other ingredients such as grains, vegetables, and supplements to provide a balanced diet.

As the chicks reach the pullet stage, they start to feather out, and their protein requirements decrease. At this stage, they should be fed a grower feed that contains around 16-18% protein. This feed will support their continued growth and development, as well as help to promote healthy feathering. The pullet stage usually lasts until the birds are about 16-20 weeks old.

Once the birds reach the point-of-lay stage, which is around 20-24 weeks old, their protein requirements decrease even further. At this stage, they should be fed a layer feed that contains around 16% protein and is fortified with calcium to support egg production. This feed will help to support the birds' overall health and well-being, and will also help to promote healthy egg production.

In addition to the protein requirements, chickens at different life stages also have different energy requirements. Chicks require more energy to support their rapid growth, while adult chickens require less energy as they are not growing as rapidly. The energy requirements of chickens can also vary depending on the temperature and their level of activity.

It's important to note that the feeding needs of chickens can also vary depending on their breed. Some breeds have different growth rates and nutritional requirements, so it's important to consult with a veterinarian or poultry nutritionist to ensure that you are providing your chickens with the proper nutrition.

1. **Rhode Island Reds:** Rhode Island Reds are a hardy and productive breed that are well-suited to backyard flocks. During the chick stage, they require a high-protein diet that is specifically formulated for chicks. This should contain at least 20-22% protein and be fortified with essential vitamins and minerals. Good protein sources for Rhode Island **Reds during this stage include soybean meal, fish meal, and meat and bone meal.**

2. **Leghorn:** Leghorns are a fast-growing and hardy breed that is well-suited for backyard flocks. During the chick stage, they require a high-protein diet that is specifically formulated for chicks. This should contain at least 20-22% protein and be fortified with essential vitamins and minerals. Good protein sources for Leghorns during this stage include soybean meal, fish meal, and meat and bone meal.

3. **Plymouth Rock:** Plymouth Rocks are a friendly and hardy breed that are well-suited for backyard flocks. During the chick stage, they require a high-protein diet that is specifically formulated for chicks. This should contain at least 20-22% protein and be fortified with essential vitamins and minerals. Good protein sources for Plymouth Rocks during this stage include soybean meal, fish meal, and meat and bone meal.

4. **Orpingtons:** Orpingtons are a friendly and hardy breed that are well-suited for backyard flocks. During the chick stage, they require a high-protein diet that is specifically formulated for chicks. This should contain at least 20-22% protein and be fortified with essential vitamins and minerals. Good protein sources for Orpingtons during this stage include soybean meal, fish meal, and meat and bone meal.

5. **Sussex:** Sussex are a friendly and hardy breed that are well-suited for backyard flocks. During the chick stage, they require a high-protein diet that is specifically formulated for chicks. This should contain at least 20-22% protein and be fortified with essential vitamins and minerals. Good protein sources for Sussex during this stage include soybean meal, fish meal, and meat and bone meal.

The second stage of a chicken's life is the grower stage, which typically lasts from 6-8 weeks to around 20 weeks of age. During this stage, chickens continue to grow rapidly and their nutritional needs change. They still require a high-protein diet, but the protein content should be slightly lower than that of the chick starter feed, around 18-20%. In addition to protein, growers also require a balanced diet that includes carbohydrates, fats, vitamins, and minerals to support their growth and development.

During the grower stage, it's important to provide chickens with a balanced diet that includes a variety of ingredients to meet their nutritional needs. This may include a combination of grains such as corn, wheat, and barley, as well as protein sources such as soybean meal, fish meal, and meat and bone meal. It's also important to make sure that chickens have access to clean water at all times.

During the grower stage, these breeds of egg laying chickens have similar nutritional requirements, but there may be slight variations depending on the breed.

1. **Rhode Island Reds:** Rhode Island Reds are a hardy and hardworking breed, and during the grower stage, they require a diet that includes a balance of protein, carbohydrates, and fats to support their growth and development. They typically require a protein content of around 18-20%, and a diet that includes a variety of grains such as corn, wheat, and barley.

2. **Plymouth Rocks:** Plymouth Rocks are known for their hardiness and friendly nature. During the grower stage, they require a diet that includes a balance of protein, carbohydrates, and fats to support their growth and development. They typically require a protein content of around 18-20%, and a diet that includes a variety of grains such as corn, wheat, and barley.

3. **Leghorns:** Leghorns are a hardy and active breed, and during the grower stage, they require a diet that includes a balance of protein, carbohydrates, and fats to support their growth

and development. They typically require a protein content of around 18-20%, and a diet that includes a variety of grains such as corn, wheat, and barley.

4. **Orpingtons:** Orpingtons are a friendly and docile breed, and during the grower stage, they require a diet that includes a balance of protein, carbohydrates, and fats to support their growth and development. They typically require a protein content of around 18-20%, and a diet that includes a variety of grains such as corn, wheat, and barley.

5. **Sussex:** Sussex are a friendly and docile breed, and during the grower stage, they require a diet that includes a balance of protein, carbohydrates, and fats to support their growth and development. They typically require a protein content of around 18-20%, and a diet that includes a variety of grains such as corn, wheat, and barley.

During the third stage, chickens enter the grower stage, where they are transitioning from chicks to adult birds. At this stage, their nutritional needs change as they begin to grow more slowly and their focus shifts from growth to maintenance. The protein content in the diet should be reduced to around 16-18%, while the energy content should remain the same. This stage usually lasts for 8-12 weeks.

1. **Rhode Island Reds:** During the grower stage, they require a diet that contains less protein than during the chick stage, but still contains essential vitamins and minerals. Good protein sources for Rhode Island Reds during this stage include soybean meal and fish meal.

2. **Leghorn:** During the grower stage, their protein needs decrease, and they require a diet that contains around 16-18% protein. Good protein sources for Leghorns during this stage include soybean meal and fish meal.

3. **Plymouth Rock:** During the grower stage, their protein needs decrease and they require a diet that contains around

16-18% protein. Good protein sources for Plymouth Rocks during this stage include soybean meal and fish meal.

4. **Orpingtons:** During the grower stage, their protein needs decrease and they require a diet that contains around 16-18% protein. Good protein sources for Orpingtons during this stage include soybean meal and fish meal.

5. **Sussex:** During the grower stage, their protein needs decrease and they require a diet that contains around 16-18% protein. Good protein sources for Sussex during this stage include soybean meal and fish meal.

The fourth stage in the lifecycle of chickens is the lay stage, which typically begins at around 18-20 weeks of age and lasts until the chickens reach the end of their productive years. During this stage, chickens will begin to lay eggs, and their diet should be formulated to support egg production. This typically includes a higher calcium content, as well as other minerals and vitamins essential for egg production.

It's necessary to provide the chickens with a balanced diet that includes a variety of nutrients. This includes protein, carbohydrates, fat, vitamins, and minerals. The protein content should be around 16-18%, carbohydrates around 3-5%, and fat around 3-4%. You also need a good source of calcium such as crushed eggshells should also be provided for the chickens to support eggshell production. It's also important to keep in mind that different breeds of chickens may have different nutritional requirements, so it's best to consult a veterinarian or poultry specialist for specific recommendations for your flock.

1. **Rhode Island Reds:** Rhode Island Reds are a hardy and productive breed that are well-suited to backyard flocks. During the lay stage, they require a diet that is formulated to support egg production. This should contain at least 16-18%

protein and be fortified with essential vitamins and minerals, including calcium. Good protein sources for Rhode Island Reds during this stage include soybean meal, fish meal, and meat and bone meal. It's also important to provide them with a source of calcium such as crushed eggshells.

2. **Leghorn:** Leghorns are a fast-growing and hardy breed that is well-suited for backyard flocks. During the lay stage, they require a diet that is formulated to support egg production. This should contain at least 16-18% protein and be fortified with essential vitamins and minerals, including calcium. Good protein sources for Leghorns during this stage include soybean meal, fish meal, and meat and bone meal. It's also important to provide them with a source of calcium such as crushed eggshells.

3. **Plymouth Rock:** Plymouth Rocks are a friendly and hardy breed that are well-suited for backyard flocks. During the lay stage, they require a diet that is formulated to support egg production. This should contain at least 16-18% protein and be fortified with essential vitamins and minerals, including calcium. Good protein sources for Plymouth Rocks during this stage include soybean meal, fish meal, and meat and bone meal. It's also **important to provide them with a source of calcium such as crushed eggshells.**

4. **Orpingtons:** Orpingtons are a friendly and hardy breed that are well-suited for backyard flocks. During the lay stage, they require a diet that is formulated to support egg production. This should contain at least 16-18% protein and be fortified with essential vitamins and minerals, including calcium. Good protein sources for Orpingtons during this stage include soybean meal, fish meal, and meat as well as bonemeal.

5. Sussex: Sussex are a friendly and hardy breed that are well-suited for backyard flocks. During the grower stage, they require a diet with a protein content of around 16-18%. This feed should also be fortified with essential vitamins and minerals. Good protein sources for Sussex during this stage include soybean meal, fish meal, and meat and bone meal. In

addition to protein, Sussex also require a source of carbohydrates for energy, such as corn, wheat, and barley. They also require a source of fat for overall health, such as vegetable oil or animal fat.

Chapter 2: Basic Feed Recipes for each stage

In this chapter, we will cover the basics of homemade chicken feed recipes. From whole grain feeds to specialized mixes for different stages of a chicken's life, there are many options to choose from. We will also discuss the benefits and drawbacks of different types of feed, as well as provide a few basic recipes to get you started.

1. **Whole Grain Chicken Feed:** This is the most basic type of chicken feed and is made from a mixture of whole grains such as corn, wheat, barley, and oats. This type of feed is perfect for backyard flocks and provides a balanced diet for chickens of all ages.

2. **Scratch Feed:** Scratch feed is a type of supplementary feed that is high in protein and is usually made from a mixture of grains, such as corn and wheat. It is typically fed as a treat to chickens and is perfect for encouraging foraging behavior.

3. **Crumble Feed:** Crumble feed is a type of feed that is made from a mixture of grains and is broken down into small, easy-to-eat pieces. This type of feed is perfect for chickens of all ages, but is particularly useful for chicks and young birds as it is easy for them to eat.

4. **Mash Feed:** Mash feed is a type of feed that is made by mixing grains with water to create a wet, porridge-like consistency. This type of feed is perfect for chickens of all ages and is particularly useful for birds that have trouble eating dry feed.

5. **Pellet Feed:** Pellet feed is a type of feed that is made by compressing grains and other ingredients together to form small pellets. This type of feed is perfect for chickens of all

ages, but is particularly useful for birds that are prone to wasting feed.

These are just a few basic feed recipes to get you started. In the following sections, we will provide more detailed recipes and discuss the benefits and drawbacks of each type of feed.

Chick Stage Recipes:

Whole Grain Chicken Feed Recipe for the entire chick stage (6-8 weeks) for a small flock of 15 chickens:

Ingredients:

- 15 pounds of whole wheat
- 10 pounds of rolled oats
- 5 pounds of barley
- 5 pounds of corn
- 2 pounds of soybean meal
- 1 pound of bone meal
- 1 pound of kelp meal
- 1/2 cup of oyster shell (for calcium)
- 1/2 cup of grit (for digestion)
- 1/4 cup of diatomaceous earth (for parasite control)

Instructions:

1. In a large mixing bowl, combine the whole wheat, rolled oats, barley, and corn.
2. In a separate mixing bowl, combine the soybean meal, bone meal, kelp meal, oyster shell, grit, and diatomaceous earth.
3. Slowly add the dry ingredient mixture to the grain mixture, stirring well to ensure that it is evenly distributed.
4. Store the feed in a cool, dry place, such as a sealed container or bag.

5. Feed to your chicks for the first 6-8 weeks of their life, using a feeder that is accessible to them at all times.
6. Keep an eye on your chicks and adjust the amount of feed you give them as needed.

Note: This recipe can be adjusted based on the specific nutritional needs of your flock, and you can consult with a veterinarian or a poultry nutritionist for more information. Additionally, this recipe will last for 1 month for a small flock of 15 chickens during the chick stage.

Chick Stage Scratch Feed:

Chick scratch feed for the entire chick stage (6-8 weeks) for a small flock of 15 chickens:

Ingredients:

- 10 lbs of whole wheat
- 5 lbs of rolled oats
- 2.5 lbs of barley
- 2.5 lbs of corn
- 2.5 lbs of sunflower seeds (optional)
- 2.5 lbs of pumpkin seeds (optional)
- 2 cups of flaxseed (optional)

Instructions:

1. In a large mixing bowl or container, combine the whole wheat, rolled oats, barley, and corn. Mix well.
2. If desired, add sunflower seeds, pumpkin seeds, and flaxseed to the mixture and mix well.
3. Store the feed in an airtight container in a cool, dry place.

4. Feed the scratch to the chicks according to the recommended daily intake.

Note: The above recipes are a basic guide and can be adjusted to suit your specific flock's needs and preferences.

Chick Stage Crumble Feed:

Crumble Feed Recipe for the entire chick stage (6-8 weeks) for a small flock of 15 chickens:

Ingredients:

- 20 lb of whole wheat or corn
- 3 lb of soybean meal
- 2 lb of fish meal
- 1 lb of bone meal
- 1/4 cup of oyster shells (ground)
- 2 tbsp of kelp meal (optional)
- 1/2 cup of a premixed poultry vitamin and mineral supplement

Instructions:

1. In a large mixing bowl, combine the whole wheat or corn, soybean meal, fish meal, and bone meal. Mix well.
2. Add in the oyster shells, kelp meal (if using), and premixed poultry vitamin and mineral supplement. Mix until well combined.
3. Use a feed grinder or food processor to grind the mixture into a crumble consistency.
4. Store the finished feed in an airtight container in a cool, dry place.
5. Feed the crumble feed to your chicks for the first 6-8 weeks of their life, along with fresh water and a source of calcium such as crushed eggshells or oyster shells. Note: It's always

recommended to check with a veterinarian or animal nutritionist for specific dietary needs and adjustments for your flock based on their age, breed, and living conditions.

Chick Stage Mash Feed:

Chick Mash Feed Recipe for the entire chick stage (6-8 weeks) for a small flock of 15 chickens:

Ingredients:

- 40 lbs of whole wheat
- 20 lbs of barley
- 20 lbs of oats
- 20 lbs of corn
- 10 lbs of soybean meal
- 2 lbs of limestone
- 2 lbs of oyster shell
- 2 lbs of kelp meal
- 1 lb of vitamin and mineral premix

Instructions:

1. In a large mixing bowl, combine the whole wheat, barley, oats, and corn.
2. In a separate bowl, mix the soybean meal, limestone, oyster shell, kelp meal, and vitamin and mineral premix together.
3. Gradually add the dry ingredients to the wet ingredients, mixing well to ensure everything is evenly distributed.
4. Store the feed in an airtight container in a cool, dry place until ready to use.
5. Feed the chicks once or twice daily, as much as they will eat in a 15 20 minute period.

Note: This recipe is formulated to provide all the necessary protein, energy and nutrients needed for the chick stage of growth and development, which typically lasts for 6-8 weeks. It is important to monitor the growth and development of your chicks and adjust their feed accordingly. It is also important to provide them with clean water at all times.

Chick Stage Pellet Feed for the entire chick stage (6-8 weeks) for a small flock of 15 chickens:

Ingredients:

- 10 lbs of whole wheat
- 5 lbs of barley
- 5 lbs of oats
- 2 lbs of soybean meal
- 2 lbs of fish meal
- 1 lb of meat and bone meal
- 1/4 lb of limestone
- 1/4 lb of oyster shell
- 1/4 lb of salt
- 1/4 lb of vitamin and mineral premix

Instructions:

1. In a large mixing bowl, combine the whole wheat, barley, and oats.
2. In a separate bowl, mix together the soybean meal, fish meal, and meat and bone meal.
3. Add the protein mixture to the grain mixture and mix well.
4. Add the limestone, oyster shell, salt, and vitamin and mineral premix to the mixture and mix well.
5. The mixture should be moist enough to hold together when pressed but not too wet. If the mixture is too dry, add small amounts of water until the desired consistency is reached.
6. Run the mixture through a pellet mill or a meat grinder with a small die attachment.

7. Allow the pellets to cool and dry before storing in an airtight container.
8. Feed the pellets to the chicks in a hopper or feeder and provide fresh water at all times.

Note: It is important to source ingredients from reputable suppliers and to store the feed in a cool, dry place to maintain its freshness and nutritional value. The feed should be stored in an airtight container and used within 3 months.

Lay Stage Recipes:

Whole Grain Chicken Feed Recipe (for Lay Stage, enough to last 1 month)

Ingredients:

- 20 lbs of whole wheat
- 10 lbs of corn
- 5 lbs of oats
- 5 lbs of barley
- 2 lbs of flaxseed
- 2 lbs of fish meal (for added protein)
- 2 lbs of kelp meal (for added minerals)
- 1 lb of oyster shell (for added calcium)

Instructions:

1. In a large mixing bowl, combine the wheat, corn, oats, and barley. Mix well.
2. Add in the flaxseed, fish meal, kelp meal, and oyster shell. Mix until well combined.
3. Store the feed in a cool, dry place in an airtight container.

4. Feed to your laying hens according to their daily needs, making sure to always have fresh feed available.
5. This recipe should last for 1 month for a small flock of 15 chickens.

Note: This recipe can be adjusted based on the size of your flock and their daily feed requirements. It is also important to regularly monitor their weight, egg production, and overall health to ensure they are receiving the proper nutrition. Also, it's a good idea to have a veterinarian check your birds every 6 months and to have their feed analyzed by a feed laboratory to ensure that you are feeding them a well-balanced diet.

Lay Stage Scratch Feed Recipe (for Lay Stage, enough to last 1 month):

Ingredients:

Ingredients:

- 25 pounds of whole wheat
- 5 pounds of rolled oats
- 5 pounds of corn
- 5 pounds of barley
- 2.5 pounds of black oil sunflower seeds
- 2.5 pounds of flaxseed
- 2.5 pounds of dried mealworms or crickets (optional)

Directions:

1. In a large mixing bowl, combine the whole wheat, rolled oats, corn, barley, sunflower seeds and flaxseed.
2. If desired, add dried mealworms or crickets to the mixture.
3. Mix all the ingredients together until well combined.
4. Store the feed in a cool, dry place in an airtight container.

5. Feed to chickens in a separate feeding dish, as scratch feed is typically not fed in a feeder. Chickens will scratch through the mixture to find the grains and seeds they want to eat.
6. Provide the scratch feed in addition to a complete feed or layer feed for a balanced diet.

Note: Scratch feed should only make up a small portion of the diet, as it does not provide all the necessary nutrients for chickens in the lay stage. It is meant to be a supplement to their diet, not the sole source of nutrition.

Crumble Feed Recipe (for Lay Stage, enough to last 6-8 weeks for a small flock of 15 chickens)

Ingredients:

- 50 lbs of whole wheat
- 25 lbs of corn
- 10 lbs of oats
- 10 lbs of barley
- 5 lbs of soybean meal
- 5 lbs of bone meal
- 2 lbs of oyster shell (for added calcium)
- 1 lb of kelp meal (for added minerals)

Instructions:

1. In a large mixing bowl, combine all the dry ingredients.
2. Mix well to evenly distribute all the ingredients.
3. Grind the mixture in a feed grinder or use a rolling pin to crush the mixture into small pieces.
4. Store the crumble feed in a cool, dry place.
5. Feed the chickens the crumble feed as their main source of nutrition, along with fresh water and access to a source of grit.

Note: This recipe can be adjusted to your chickens' needs and your personal preferences. You can also add or subtract ingredients, such as adding flaxseed for added Omega-3s or switching out the wheat for another type of grain.

Mash Feed Recipe for Lay Stage (6-8 weeks worth)

Ingredients:

- 50 lbs of whole wheat
- 25 lbs of rolled oats
- 25 lbs of corn meal
- 15 lbs of barley
- 15 lbs of flaxseed
- 10 lbs of soybean meal
- 5 lbs of kelp meal
- 2.5 lbs of oyster shell
- 2.5 lbs of dicalcium phosphate
- 2.5 lbs of limestone

Instructions:

1. In a large mixing bowl, combine the whole wheat, rolled oats, corn meal, barley, and flaxseed. Mix well.
2. In a separate bowl, mix together the soybean meal, kelp meal, oyster shell, dicalcium phosphate, and limestone.
3. Slowly add the dry mineral mixture to the grain mixture, and mix well until everything is evenly distributed.
4. Store the feed in a cool, dry place, such as a barn or shed, in a sealed container or covered with a tarp to keep it fresh.
5. To feed the chickens, place the Mash Feed in a container in the coop or run, and allow the chickens to eat as much as they want. The feed should last for 6-8 weeks.

Note: If you are using a feeder, make sure it is cleaned out regularly to prevent spoilage.

Pellet Feed Recipe for Lay Stage (1 Month Supply) Ingredients:

- 50 lbs of whole wheat
- 25 lbs of barley
- 25 lbs of oats
- 10 lbs of field peas
- 5 lbs of flaxseed
- 2 lbs of limestone
- 1 lb of oyster shell
- 1 lb of salt
- 1 lb of a premixed poultry mineral supplement
- 1 lb of kelp meal (optional)

Directions:

1. In a large mixing bowl, combine the whole wheat, barley, oats, field peas, flaxseed, limestone, oyster shell, salt, mineral supplement, and kelp meal (if using). Mix well.
2. Using a feed pelletizer, turn the mixture into pellets.
3. Store the pellets in a cool, dry place, and feed to your chickens as needed.

Note: The amounts of each ingredient can be adjusted slightly depending on the nutritional needs of your flock and the availability of ingredients. It's important to consult with a poultry nutritionist to ensure that your chickens are getting the proper balance of nutrients. Also, always make sure to have fresh, clean water available for your chickens at all times.

Grower Stage Recipes:

Grower Stage Whole Grain Chicken Feed

Ingredients:

- 40 lbs of whole corn
- 20 lbs of whole wheat
- 20 lbs of barley
- 20 lbs of oats
- 10 lbs of soybean meal
- 5 lbs of limestone
- 5 lbs of oyster shell
- 3 lbs of kelp meal
- 2 lbs of dicalcium phosphate

Instructions:

1. Mix all ingredients together in a large container or feed bin.
2. Store in a cool, dry place to prevent spoilage.
3. Feed to your chickens as their primary source of nutrition during the grower stage, along with access to fresh water at all times.

Note: You can make adjustments to the recipe according to your chicken's specific needs and dietary requirements. It's also important to consult with a veterinarian or a poultry nutritionist to ensure that the diet you are providing is complete and balanced for your birds.

Also, the grower stage typically lasts for around 8-12 weeks, depending on the breed of chicken and the desired size at maturity.

Grower Stage Scratch Feed

Grower Stage Scratch Feed Recipe (for 15 chickens for 6-8 weeks)

Ingredients:

- 3 pounds of corn
- 2 pounds of wheat

- 1 pound of barley
- 1 pound of oats
- 1/2 pound of sunflower seeds
- 1/4 pound of flaxseed
- 1/4 pound of fishmeal (optional)

Instructions:

1. In a large mixing bowl, combine the corn, wheat, barley, oats, sunflower seeds, flaxseed, and fishmeal (if using). Mix well to combine all the ingredients.
2. Store the scratch feed in an airtight container to keep it fresh.
3. Offer the scratch feed to your chickens in a separate feeder from their regular feed, as a treat or supplement to their diet.

Note: These measurements are approximate and can be adjusted to suit your specific flock's needs and preferences. Also, Scratch feed should not be the only feed given to chickens, it should be offered as a treat or supplement to a balanced diet.

Grower Stage Whole Grain Chicken Feed

Ingredients:

- 50 lbs of whole wheat
- 25 lbs of whole corn
- 15 lbs of oats
- 10 lbs of barley
- 5 lbs of flaxseed
- 3 lbs of kelp meal (provides essential minerals)
- 2 lbs of oyster shell (provides calcium)
- 1 lb of bone meal (provides phosphorus)
- 1 lb of salt (provides necessary sodium)

Instructions:

1. Start by mixing all of the dry ingredients together in a large container or bin.
2. Stir the mixture thoroughly to ensure that all ingredients are evenly distributed.
3. Store the feed in an airtight container, in a cool and dry place.

This recipe should make enough feed for 15 chickens for approximately 8-10 weeks during the grower stage. It is important to monitor the chickens' weight and health to ensure they are getting the proper nutrition, and make adjustments to the feed as necessary.

Grower Stage Scratch Feed

Grower Stage Scratch Feed Recipe (for 15 chickens):

- 2 pounds of whole wheat
- 1 pound of barley
- 1 pound of oats
- 1 pound of corn
- 1/2 pound of sunflower seeds
- 1/4 pound of flaxseed (optional)
- 1/4 cup of powdered limestone (for added calcium)

Instructions:

1. Mix all ingredients together in a large container.
2. Store in an airtight container in a cool, dry place.
3. Feed as a supplement to the chickens' regular diet, offering about 1/4 cup per chicken per day.
4. This recipe should last for about 4-6 weeks for a small flock of 15 chickens.

Crumble Feed

Grower Stage Crumble Feed Recipe (for 15 chickens for 6-8 weeks) Ingredients:

- 50 pounds of corn
- 25 pounds of barley
- 25 pounds of oats
- 10 pounds of wheat
- 2 cups of limestone
- 1 cup of oyster shell
- 1 cup of salt
- 1/2 cup of poultry vitamins and minerals
- 1/4 cup of kelp meal (optional)

Instructions:

1. In a large mixing bowl, combine the corn, barley, oats, and wheat.
2. In a separate bowl, mix together the limestone, oyster shell, salt, poultry vitamins and minerals, and kelp meal (if using).
3. Add the dry ingredients from step 2 to the grain mixture in step 1 and mix well.
4. Use a feed grinder or a food processor to grind the ingredients into a crumble consistency.
5. Store in an airtight container in a cool, dry place.
6. Feed to the chickens in conjunction with fresh water and free-range access to insects and greens.

Note: These recipes make enough feed for 15 chickens for 6-8 weeks in the grower stage. Adjust the ingredients accordingly for larger or smaller flocks or for a longer or shorter time period.

Mash Feed

Grower Stage Mash Feed Recipe (for 15 chickens for 6-8 weeks)

Ingredients:

- 25 pounds of whole wheat
- 12.5 pounds of corn
- 12.5 pounds of barley
- 5 pounds of soybean meal
- 2.5 pounds of limestone
- 2.5 pounds of oyster shell
- 2.5 pounds of salt

Instructions:

1. Mix all ingredients together in a large container or feed mixer.
2. Store the feed in an airtight container to maintain freshness.
3. Feed to chickens as needed, about 1 pound of feed per chicken per day.

Note: This recipe is formulated to provide all the necessary nutrients for the chickens during the grower stage.

Chapter 3: Advanced Feed Recipes

Organic Chicken Feed: Organic chicken feed is a type of feed that is made with ingredients that are grown and processed without the use of synthetic pesticides, fertilizers, or genetically modified organisms (GMOs). This type of feed is considered more sustainable and environmentally friendly than conventional feed, as it supports organic farming practices and reduces the amount of harmful chemicals that are used in the production of feed ingredients.

There are many benefits to choosing organic chicken feed over conventional feed. One of the main benefits is that organic feed is considered healthier for chickens, as it is free from synthetic chemicals and GMOs that can be harmful to chickens and may negatively impact their health. Organic feed is also considered more nutritious, as it is made with high-quality ingredients that are rich in vitamins, minerals, and other essential nutrients.

Another benefit of organic chicken feed is that it is better for the environment. Organic farming practices are known to improve soil health, conserve water, and reduce pollution and greenhouse gas emissions. By choosing organic feed, chicken farmers can help to promote sustainable agriculture and reduce the environmental impact of their operations.

In terms of cost, organic chicken feed is typically more expensive than conventional feed. This is due to the higher cost of organic ingredients and the additional labor and certifications required to produce organic feed. However, many chicken farmers who choose to use organic feed believe that the benefits to their chickens' health and the environment outweigh the additional cost.

Non-GMO Chicken Feed: Non-GMO chicken feed is made from ingredients that are not genetically modified. This means that the feed is free from GMOs, which are organisms whose genetic makeup has been altered in a way that does not occur naturally. Non-GMO feed is generally considered to be healthier and more sustainable than feed made from GMOs.

One of the main reasons for choosing non-GMO chicken feed is that it is free from the potential negative health effects of GMOs. Some studies have suggested that GMOs may cause health problems for animals, including chickens, although more research is needed to confirm these findings. Additionally, non-GMO feed is more environmentally friendly as it does not contribute to the proliferation of GMOs.

Another plus for non-GMO feed is that it is often more nutritious than feed made from GMOs. Non-GMO ingredients are less likely to have been treated with pesticides or other chemicals, which can lead to higher nutrient content in the feed. However, non-GMO feed can also be more expensive than conventional feed, as the cost of producing non-GMO ingredients is often higher. This can be a deterrent for some farmers, but for those who prioritize the health and welfare of their chickens, the added cost may be worth it.

It is important to note that organic feed does not always mean non-GMO feed, and vice versa.

Benefits of feeding your chickens Non-GMO feed:

- Avoiding the potential health risks associated with genetically modified ingredients.
- Supporting sustainable farming practices and protecting the environment.
- Helping to maintain the genetic diversity of crops.

Non-GMO Chicken Feed Recipe

Ingredients:

Ingredients:

- 25 lbs of Organic Whole Wheat
- 15 lbs of Organic Cracked Corn
- 10 lbs of Organic Dried Beans (such as navy or pinto)
- 5 lbs of Organic Rolled Oats
- 2 lbs of Organic Flaxseed
- 2 lbs of Organic Sunflower Seeds
- 1 lb of Organic Kelp Meal
- 1 lb of Organic Oyster Shells (for added calcium)
- 1 lb of Organic Dried Mealworms (optional, for added protein)

Instructions:

1. In a large mixing bowl, combine the whole wheat, cracked corn, dried beans, rolled oats, flaxseed, and sunflower seeds. Mix well.
2. Add in the kelp meal, oyster shells, and dried mealworms (if using). Mix again until everything is evenly distributed.
3. Store the feed in a cool, dry place, and use it within a month.

It is important to acknowledge that while organic feed is a good choice for many chicken keepers, it may not be the best option for every situation. It is always recommended to do your own research and consult with a veterinarian or poultry expert before making any changes to your chicken's diet.

Note: This recipe yields approximately 100 pounds of Non-GMO chicken feed and should last for about 4-6 weeks for a small flock of 15 chickens. Adjust the amounts accordingly for a larger flock. You can turn any of the aforementioned recipes in the previous chapter in to organic by changing the ingredients to organic, just be aware that there is a cost difference.

Soy-Free and Corn-Free Feed Recipes

For chickens that are sensitive to soy or corn, or for those who want to avoid genetically modified ingredients, soy-free and corn-free feed recipes are a great option. These recipes typically use alternative protein sources such as peas, beans, and sunflower seeds, and can be made with whole grains such as oats and barley. You can substitute as you wish and experiment with what works best for your flock.

Grower Feeds

Grower feeds are specially formulated to provide the balanced nutrition that chickens need during the key growth stages, typically between 4 to 18 weeks of age. These feeds typically contain higher levels of protein to support muscle and tissue development, as well as essential amino acids, vitamins, and minerals to support overall growth and health.

As we have covered, grower feeds contain around 18-20% protein and are formulated to meet the nutritional requirements of the birds during this stage of growth. They are often formulated with a variety of ingredients including whole grains such as corn, barley, and oats, as well as protein sources such as soybeans, fish meal, and animal by-products. Some grower feeds may also include added probiotics and enzymes to support gut health and digestion.

It is important to remember that some growers may prefer to use non-GMO or organic ingredients in their grower feeds. These can be more expensive, but some farmers believe that these options provide better nutrition and may be more sustainable for the environment.

You should also note that when using grower feeds, it is important to monitor the birds' growth and adjust the feed accordingly. As the birds reach the end of the grower stage, they will need to be gradually transitioned to a layer or broiler feed to ensure they receive the proper nutrition for their next stage of life.

Layer Feeds

Layer feeds are specially formulated to meet the nutritional needs of chickens that are actively laying eggs. These feeds typically contain higher levels of protein and calcium to support the growth and maintenance of strong eggshells. They also often contain added vitamins and minerals to support overall health and egg production. Some layer feed recipes may also include added sources of essential fatty acids, such as flaxseed or fish oil, to support the health of the chickens' reproductive systems.

It is important to note that layer feeds should not be fed to chickens that are not yet laying eggs, as the high levels of calcium can cause harm to the birds' kidneys and other organs. Additionally, it is important to monitor the protein levels in layer feed, as too much protein can lead to reduced egg production. Many commercial layer feeds are formulated to be fed to chickens starting at 18-20 weeks of age or when the birds start to lay eggs.

When making your own layer feed, it is important to use high-quality, non-GMO ingredients, and to carefully measure and mix the feed to ensure that the chickens are receiving the appropriate balance of nutrients. Some common ingredients in homemade layer feed recipes include whole grains, such as corn, barley, and oats, as well as legumes, such as peas, beans, and soybeans. It's also important to add crushed eggshells or oyster shells as a source of calcium. Additionally, it is a good idea to include a source of essential fatty acids, such as flaxseed or fish oil, in your layer feed recipe.

Broiler Feeds

Broiler feed is a type of chicken feed that is specifically formulated for chickens that are being raised for meat production. These feeds are typically higher in protein and energy than other types of chicken feed, as the birds need these nutrients to grow quickly and efficiently. Some common ingredients found in broiler feed include corn, soybeans, and fishmeal. These ingredients provide the birds with the necessary energy and protein to support their rapid growth. Additionally, broiler feed may also contain added vitamins and minerals to support the birds' overall health and well-being.

It is also important to note that different stages of broiler growth require different types of feed. For example, starter feed is typically used for the first 4-6 weeks of life, while grower feed is used for the next 4-6 weeks, and finisher feed is used for the final 2-4 weeks before harvest. The nutritional composition of each type of feed is tailored to meet the specific needs of the birds at each stage of growth.

When feeding broiler chickens, it is important to provide them with access to clean, fresh water at all times. Additionally, it is important to monitor their growth and adjust their feed accordingly. Overfeeding can lead to health problems and increased feed costs, while underfeeding can slow growth and reduce meat yield. Proper feeding management is crucial for achieving optimal growth and meat production in broiler chickens.

Chapter 4: Feeding Strategies

Free-Range Feeding - Free-range feeding is a popular method for raising chickens in which the birds are allowed to forage for their own food in a large outdoor area. This method is not only more natural for the chickens, but it also allows them to exercise and get fresh air. When using this method, it is important to make sure that the chickens have access to a balanced diet, including a variety of grains, greens, and insects.

This can be accomplished by providing a mix of scratch feed, whole grain feed, and supplementary protein sources such as mealworms or crickets. Free-range feeding is a method of raising chickens where they are allowed to roam and forage for their own food, as opposed to being confined to a coop or pen. This method of feeding has several benefits for both the chickens and the farmer.

First, free-range chickens are able to forage for a variety of foods, including insects, seeds, and greens, which can provide them with a more balanced and varied diet than a commercial feed alone. This can lead to healthier chickens with stronger immune systems and fewer health problems.

Free-range feeding also allows chickens to engage in natural behaviors such as dust bathing, scratching, and foraging, which can improve their overall well-being and reduce stress.

Additionally, free-range feeding can be more cost-effective for farmers. By allowing chickens to forage for their own food, farmers can reduce the amount of commercial feed they need to purchase, as well as reduce the amount of waste that needs to be disposed of.

However, there are also some challenges to free-range feeding. Chickens need to be protected from predators, so farmers must take steps to secure the coop and fencing to keep the chickens safe. Additionally, chickens can cause damage to gardens and landscaping if they are not supervised, so farmers must be prepared to manage the chickens' access to different areas of the property.

In addition to the benefits of allowing chickens to forage for their own food and the potential cost savings, free-range feeding also allows chickens to engage in natural behaviors such as dust bathing and foraging. This can lead to a healthier and happier flock. However, it is important to note that free-range feeding also has its drawbacks, such as increased predation risk and the possibility of disease transmission from wild birds. It is also important to ensure that the chickens have access to a secure coop at night to protect them from predators.

It's also good to note that free-range feeding may not be suitable for all farmers, depending on the size of their property, the number of chickens they have, and the local climate. However, for those who have the resources and are willing to put in the extra effort, free-range feeding can be a great option for raising healthy and happy chickens.

Feeding for Optimal Health - In order to keep chickens healthy, it is important to provide them with a balanced diet that includes all the necessary vitamins, minerals, and amino acids. A diet that is high in protein and low in fat is best for maintaining optimal health. Whole grains such as corn, barley, and oats provide chickens with the necessary carbohydrates and fiber, while legumes such as peas, beans, and soybeans provide protein. It is also important to provide chickens with a source of calcium, such as crushed eggshells or oyster shells, to support strong eggshells and bone growth. Feeding for optimal health is an essential aspect of raising chickens. A balanced diet that provides all the necessary nutrients and vitamins is essential for maintaining the overall health and well-being of your birds.

One important consideration when feeding for optimal health is protein. Chickens require a high-quality protein source in their diet, such as soybeans, fish meal, or meat meal. A protein deficiency can lead to poor growth, feather loss, and a weakened immune system.

Another important nutrient for optimal health is calcium. Chickens need calcium for strong bones and egg production. Good sources of calcium include crushed eggshells, oyster shell, or limestone. It is important to note that if you are using crushed eggshells as a calcium source, they should be thoroughly cleaned and baked to remove any bacteria before giving to your birds.

Vitamins and minerals are also important for optimal health. Chickens require a variety of vitamins and minerals, including vitamins A, D3, and E, as well as the minerals zinc and selenium. These can be found in a variety of sources such as kelp, alfalfa meal, or premixes specifically formulated for chickens.

Lastly, it is essential to provide clean, fresh water for your chickens at all times. It is also important to make sure that the water does not freeze during the winter months.

Feeding for optimal health requires providing a balanced diet that includes a good source of protein, calcium, vitamins and minerals, and clean, fresh water. It is important to consult a veterinarian or a nutritionist to ensure that your chickens are getting the proper nutrition they need.

Feeding for Egg Production - To maximize egg production, chickens need a diet that is high in protein, calcium, and essential fatty acids. Whole grains such as corn, barley, and oats provide carbohydrates and fiber, while legumes such as peas, beans, and soybeans provide protein. To increase calcium intake, chickens can be offered crushed eggshells or oyster shells. In addition, chickens that are laying eggs need a source of essential fatty acids, such as flaxseed or fish oil. To maximize egg production, it is important to understand the nutritional requirements of chickens.

Chickens need a diet that is high in protein, calcium, and essential fatty acids. These nutrients are crucial for the development and maintenance of strong shells for eggs. Whole grains such as corn, barley, and oats provide carbohydrates and fiber, which are important for overall health and energy. Legumes such as peas, beans, and soybeans are high in protein, which is essential for egg production.

Calcium is also important for egg production, as it is needed to form strong eggshells. Chickens can obtain calcium from their feed, but they may also need a supplementary source such as crushed eggshells or oyster shells. These can be offered in a separate dish or mixed in with the feed.

In addition, chickens that are laying eggs need a source of essential fatty acids, such as flaxseed or fish oil. Essential fatty acids are important for overall health and can also improve egg production by increasing the size and quality of eggs. These can be added to the feed or offered as a separate supplement. It's also important to note that chickens need access to clean fresh water at all times, and that the feed should be stored in a dry and cool place to prevent spoilage and mold. It is recommended to consult with a veterinarian or a poultry nutritionist to make sure that the chickens are getting the right balance of nutrients based on the specific needs of the flock.

Other strategies that can be used to promote and boost quality egg production include:

- Providing chickens with access to natural sunlight or artificial light to help regulate their laying cycle and increase the number of eggs laid
- Ensuring that chickens have access to clean and fresh water at all times
- Managing the flock to prevent overcrowding and maintain a healthy population density
- Avoiding stress and providing a comfortable and safe living environment for the chickens
- Regularly monitoring the health of the chickens and addressing any issues that arise quickly to minimize disruptions in egg production
- Being very consistent and balanced feeding program that meets the nutritional needs of the chickens, including providing appropriate amounts of protein, calcium, and essential fatty acids.
- Providing additional supplements such as probiotics, vitamins, and minerals to support the overall health of the chickens.
- Using breeds that are known for their high egg production.
- Provide nesting box and encourage the hens to lay eggs in it
- Maintaining optimal temperature, humidity and ventilation in the coop
- Managing the flock to minimize predators and disease pressure
- Proper feeding management, like feeding the right feed at the right time.

Feeding for Meat Production - To produce meat, chickens need a diet that is high in protein and energy. Whole grains such as corn, barley, and oats provide the necessary carbohydrates and fiber, while legumes such as peas, beans, and soybeans provide protein. In addition, chickens that are being raised for meat should be fed a diet that is high in energy, such as a diet that includes added fat or oil. When raising chickens for meat production, the main focus is on promoting rapid growth and muscle development. To achieve this, a diet high in protein is essential. Whole grains such as corn, barley, and oats provide carbohydrates and energy, while protein sources such as soybeans, fish meal, or meat and bone meal provide the necessary amino acids for muscle growth. In addition, chickens raised for meat production should also be provided with a source of essential fatty acids, such as flaxseed or fish oil, to support overall health and growth.

Another important aspect of feeding for meat production is monitoring feed intake and body weight. Chickens that are growing too slowly may need to be provided with a higher protein diet, while chickens that are growing too quickly may need to be switched to a lower protein diet to prevent leg problems.

It's also important to note that chickens raised for meat production should be provided with plenty of space and access to the outdoors to promote physical activity, which will help to build muscle and overall health. They should also be provided with a balanced diet that includes vitamins and minerals, which support the overall growth and development.

Furthermore, it is important to consider the stage of growth when formulating a diet for meat production, as chickens of different ages have different nutritional requirements. For example, broiler chickens require a higher protein diet than older chickens, whereas older chickens require a diet that is lower in protein but higher in energy.

Other strategies for maximizing meat production include:

1. **Feeding a high-protein diet:** Chickens that are being raised for meat production require a diet that is high in protein to support muscle growth. This can be achieved by including ingredients such as soybeans, fishmeal, or meat and bone meal in the feed.

2. **Gradual Increase in Feed:** Gradually increasing the amount of feed given to chickens as they grow is an effective strategy for maximizing meat production. This allows the chickens to gradually adapt to the increased nutrient needs associated with growth.

3. **Proper Culling:** Culling birds that are not meeting production standards or are not growing at the same rate as the rest of the flock can help to optimize meat production. This ensures that resources are not being wasted on birds that are unlikely to reach their full potential.

4. **Proper Feeding Schedule:** Feeding chickens on a consistent schedule can help to optimize meat production. This ensures that the birds are receiving the necessary nutrients at the right time, which can help to promote efficient growth.

5. **Addition of Supplements:** Adding supplements such as vitamins and minerals to the feed can help to optimize meat production. This can help to ensure that chickens are receiving all of the necessary nutrients to support growth and health.

6. **Monitor Body Condition:** Monitoring the body condition of chickens regularly can help to identify issues that may be impacting meat production. This can include things like parasite infestations, disease, or poor nutrition, which can then be addressed to optimize meat production.

7. **Proper Lighting:** Providing chickens with the proper lighting can help to optimize meat production. This can include providing longer daylight hours, which can help to stimulate growth, or providing artificial lighting to extend the day length.

In conclusion, feeding strategies play a crucial role in the health, growth, and production of chickens. Free-range feeding allows chickens to forage for their own food, which can improve their overall health and well-being. Feeding for optimal health involves providing a balanced diet with the right combination of nutrients and supplements. Feeding for egg production requires a diet high in protein, calcium, and essential fatty acids, as well as providing a source of calcium through crushed eggshells or oyster shells.

Feeding for meat production requires a diet high in protein and energy, as well as strategies such as controlling the amount of feed and providing adequate exercise to promote muscle development. These strategies, when implemented correctly, can help to maximize production and improve the overall quality of eggs and meat produced by the chickens.

Chapter 5: Supplementing Feed

In addition to providing a well-balanced diet, chickens can benefit from supplementing their feed with a variety of items. These supplements can provide extra nutrition and help to keep chickens healthy and productive.

Kitchen Scraps: Chickens are opportunistic eaters and will happily consume a wide variety of kitchen scraps. Kitchen scraps can be a great supplement to a chicken's diet, providing them with a variety of vitamins and minerals. Some of the best kitchen scraps to feed chickens include vegetable scraps, fruit scraps, and bread. However, it is important to avoid feeding chickens any scraps that are moldy or spoiled, as well as any scraps that contain high levels of sugar or fat, such as cake or french fries.

When feeding chickens kitchen scraps, it is best to chop or grind them up into small pieces to make it easier for the chickens to eat. You can also mix the scraps in with their regular feed to make sure they get a balanced diet.

It is also important to note that while kitchen scraps can be a great supplement to a chicken's diet, they should not make up the majority of their diet. Chickens still require a balanced, nutrient-rich feed to stay healthy and produce eggs or meat.

Greens and Herbs: Chickens love fresh greens and herbs, and they can provide a valuable source of vitamins and minerals. Greens and herbs can be a valuable supplement to a chicken's diet, providing a source of vitamins, minerals, and other nutrients. Some examples of greens and herbs that can be fed to chickens include lettuce, spinach, kale, dandelion greens, parsley, and basil. These can be fed fresh or dried. Chickens also enjoy foraging for greens and herbs in the garden or pasture. Adding a variety of greens and herbs to a chicken's diet can also help to keep them healthy and prevent boredom. Some popular herbs that can be fed to chickens include rosemary, thyme, and oregano which are known for their anti-inflammatory and antioxidant properties. Additionally, mint and basil are great for promoting healthy digestion. It is important to note that while chickens can eat a variety of greens and herbs, some plants can be toxic to chickens such as avocado, rhubarb leaves and tomato leaves.

In addition to providing a source of vitamins and minerals, greens and herbs can also offer other health benefits for chickens. For example, certain herbs such as thyme and oregano have antimicrobial properties that can help to boost the immune system and protect against disease. Greens such as kale and spinach are high in calcium, which is essential for healthy eggshells. Other greens such as lettuce and cabbage can provide a source of hydration, which is especially important in hot weather. When offering greens and herbs to chickens, it's important to make sure that they are fresh and free of pesticides or other chemicals. Chickens will also enjoy foraging for greens and herbs in a supervised free-range area.

Protein Supplements: Chickens require a diet that is high in protein, especially during the growing and laying stages. Some good options for protein supplements include mealworms, crickets, and earthworms. These can be fed to chickens fresh, or they can be dried and included in the feed. Protein supplements are a great way to boost the protein content in a chicken's diet. Some common protein supplements include:

1. **Soybean meal:** Made from roasted soybeans, soybean meal is a high-quality protein source that is often used in commercial chicken feed.

2. **Fish meal:** Fish meal is made from cooked, dried, and ground fish and is an excellent source of protein, omega-3 fatty acids, and minerals.

3. **Meat and bone meal:** Made from rendered animal parts, meat and bone meal is a protein-rich supplement that is high in calcium and phosphorus.

4. **Blood meal:** Made from dried, ground blood, this supplement is high in protein, iron, and other minerals.

5. **Feather meal:** Made from ground, dried poultry feathers, feather meal is a protein-rich supplement that is also high in calcium.

It is important to note that some of these protein supplements such as blood meal, meat and bone meal and feather meal may not be legal in some countries or states, and it is important to check your local laws before using them as a protein supplement. Also, it is important to check the quality of the product, as some suppliers may use low-quality ingredients that may contain harmful pathogens, and therefore it is important to use a reputable supplier.

Mineral Supplements: In addition to protein supplements, mineral supplements can also be added to a chicken's diet to ensure they are getting all the necessary nutrients. Chickens need a variety of minerals to stay healthy, including calcium, phosphorus, and sodium. Chickens can obtain these minerals from their feed, but if their diet is lacking, they can be given supplements. One good option is to provide crushed eggshells or oyster shells, which are high in calcium.

Some common mineral supplements include oyster shell, bone meal, and granite grit. These supplements can help chickens with strong eggshells and healthy bones. It is important to note that mineral supplements should always be offered separately from a chicken's regular feed, as they can interfere with the absorption of other nutrients. It is also important to note that not all mineral supplements are created equal, so it is important to research and choose a reputable brand that is specifically formulated for chickens.

Chapter 6: Troubleshooting and FAQ

Common Feeding Problems:

1. **Chickens not eating the feed:** This can come from multiple causes including a lack of variety in their diet, a dirty coop, or an improper feeding schedule. To solve this problem, try offering a variety of different types of feed, making sure the coop is clean and well-ventilated, and adjusting the feeding schedule to better suit the chickens' needs.

2. **Diarrhea:** This can be the result of a number of underlying causes., including a diet that is too high in protein or a lack of fiber. To solve this problem, try adjusting the chickens' diet to include more fiber-rich foods, such as greens and vegetables, and reducing the amount of protein-rich foods, such as meat and eggs.

3. **Crop problems:** There are various reasons for this including a lack of calcium, a lack of light, or a lack of protein. To

solve this problem, try adding crushed eggshells or oyster shells to the chickens' diet to increase their calcium intake, making sure they have access to natural light, and increasing the amount of protein-rich foods in their diet.

4. **Egg binding:** It is likely the result of several factors, including a lack of calcium, a lack of space, or a lack of exercise. To solve this problem, try adding crushed eggshells or oyster shells to the chickens' diet to increase their calcium intake, increasing their living space, and encouraging them to be more active.

5. **Feather picking:** This can be caused by a number of factors, including a lack of space, a lack of protein, or a lack of light. To solve this problem, try increasing the chickens' living space, increasing the amount of protein-rich foods in their diet, and making sure they have access to natural light.

6. **Scaly leg mite and lice:** This is a common parasite that can cause chickens to have scaly, irritated legs. This can be caused by a number of factors, including a dirty coop, a lack of clean bedding, or a lack of proper sanitation. To solve this problem, try keeping the coop clean and well-ventilated, providing fresh, clean bedding, and practicing good sanitation techniques.

7. **Worms:** The cause of this could be multifaceted. This includes a dirty coop, a lack of clean water, or a lack of proper sanitation. To solve this problem, try keeping the coop clean and well-ventilated, providing fresh, clean water at all times, and practicing good sanitation techniques.

8. **Marek's Disease:** The solution for Marek's disease is to prevent it from occurring in the first place through vaccination. The vaccine is usually given to chickens at a young age, typically around 1-2 weeks old, and can provide long-term protection against the disease. In cases where the disease has already occurred, treatment options are limited and usually involve supportive care to alleviate symptoms. In severe cases, euthanasia may be necessary to prevent suffering. Additionally, biosecurity measures such as limiting

the introduction of new birds to the flock and keeping the birds separate from wild birds can help prevent the spread of the disease.

9. **Heat Stress:** This can be caused by a number of factors, including a lack of shade, a lack of water, or a lack of proper ventilation. To solve this problem, try providing shade, making sure the chickens have access to clean, cool water, and ensuring that the coop is well-ventilated.

10. **Coccidiosis:** There are many potential reasons for this, including a dirty coop, a lack of clean water, or a lack of proper sanitation. To solve this problem, try keeping the coop clean and well-ventilated, providing fresh, clean water at all times, and practicing good sanitation techniques.

11. **Slow growth:** This can be the outcome of various causes, including a lack of protein, a lack of light, or a lack of vitamins and minerals. To solve this problem, try increasing the amount of protein-rich foods in the chickens' diet, making sure they have access to natural light, and adding a vitamin and mineral supplement to their feed

12. **Loss of appetite:** There are likely multiple contributing factors such as infection, worms, or a sudden change in diet. Solution: Consult a veterinarian to rule out any underlying health issues and ensure the chickens are on a balanced diet.

13. **Vomiting or regurgitation:** This may stem from a variety of reasons, such as infection, worms, or a sudden change in diet. Solution: Consult a veterinarian to rule out any underlying health issues and ensure the chickens are on a balanced diet.

14. **Weak eggshells:** This can be caused by a lack of calcium in the diet. Solution: Ensure the chickens have access to a source of calcium, such as crushed eggshells or oyster shells.

15. **Low egg production:** This can be caused by a lack of nutrients in the diet, or by stress. Solution: Ensure the chickens are on a balanced diet that is high in protein, calcium, and essential fatty acids and try to reduce stress in the flock.

FAQ's

Q: What are the benefits of making your own chicken feed?

A: Making your own chicken feed allows you to have control over the ingredients and nutritional content, which can lead to healthier chickens and better egg or meat production. It can also save money in the long run and reduce your reliance on commercial feed sources.

Q: What are the key ingredients in chicken feed?

A: The key ingredients in chicken feed typically include a source of carbohydrates (such as whole grains), a source of protein (such as legumes), and essential vitamins and minerals.

Q: Can I use kitchen scraps to supplement my chicken's diet?

A: Yes, kitchen scraps can be a great way to supplement your chicken's diet. However, it is important to make sure the scraps are safe for chickens to eat and that they are providing a balanced diet.

Q: Can I feed my chickens only homemade feed?

A: Yes, chickens can be fed only homemade feed, but it is important to make sure the feed is nutritionally balanced and contains all the necessary vitamins and minerals for the chickens' health.

Q: How do I know if my homemade feed is nutritionally balanced?

A: You can consult with a veterinarian or a poultry nutritionist to have the feed analyzed and ensure it is nutritionally balanced. You can also reference common feed recipes and ingredient ratios that have been tested and proven to provide a balanced diet for chickens.

Q: How often should I change my chickens' feed?

A: Chickens can be fed the same feed for a period of time, but it is recommended to rotate the feed every few months to provide a varied diet and ensure they are getting all necessary nutrients.

Q: Can I feed my chickens organic feed?

A: Yes, you can make organic feed for your chickens by using certified organic ingredients.

Q: Can I feed my chickens non-GMO feed?

A: Yes, you can make non-GMO feed for your chickens by using non-genetically modified ingredients.

Q: How can I save money when making my own chicken feed?

A: One way to save money when making your own chicken feed is to buy ingredients in bulk. You can also grow some of the ingredients yourself, such as sprouted grains or legumes, to reduce the cost.

Q: How do I store my homemade chicken feed?

A: Homemade chicken feed should be stored in a cool, dry place and in an airtight container to preserve its freshness and prevent spoilage.

Q: How long can homemade chicken feed be stored?

A: Homemade chicken feed can be stored for several months if stored properly, but it is recommended to use it within 3 months for best nutritional value.

Q: Can I feed my chickens kitchen scraps as a supplement to their regular feed?

A: Yes, chickens can eat a variety of kitchen scraps such as fruits and vegetables, bread, pasta, and cooked grains. However, it's important to avoid giving them anything that is moldy or spoiled, as well as anything that contains caffeine, alcohol, or seasonings. It's also important to note that kitchen scraps should not make up the majority of a chicken's diet and should be used as a supplement to their regular feed.

Q: Can I feed my chickens table scraps?

A: While chickens can eat table scraps, it's important to avoid giving them anything that is high in fat, salt, or sugar. Also, avoid giving them anything that contains caffeine, alcohol, or seasonings. It's also important to note that table scraps should not make up the majority of a chicken's diet and should be used as a supplement to their regular feed.

Q: Can I feed my chickens grass clippings?

A: Yes, chickens can eat grass clippings. However, it's important to make sure that the grass has not been treated with any chemicals or pesticides. Also, grass clippings should not make up the majority of a chicken's diet and should be used as a supplement to their regular feed.

Q: Can I feed my chickens weeds from my garden?

A: Yes, chickens can eat a variety of weeds, however, it's important to make sure that the weeds have not been treated with any chemicals or pesticides. Also, weeds should not make up the majority of a chicken's diet and should be used as a supplement to their regular feed.

Q: How often should I feed my chickens?

A: Chickens should have access to feed at all times. A good rule of thumb is to provide 1/4 to 1/3 pound of feed per chicken per day. The amount of feed needed will vary depending on the size of the chicken, their age, and the climate. See the feeding instructions in the earlier chapters of this book for more detail.

Q: Can I feed my chickens moldy feed?

A: No, you should never feed your chickens moldy feed as it can make them sick. Always check the feed for mold before giving it to your chickens and discard any feed that is moldy.

Q: Can I mix my own chicken feed?

A: Yes, you can mix your own chicken feed. However, it's important to make sure that the feed contains the proper balance of protein, carbohydrates, and fats. A good rule of thumb is to include a protein source, such as soybeans or corn, a carbohydrate source, such as oats or barley, and a fat source, such as flaxseed or sunflower seeds.

Q: How much feed should I give my chickens?

A: The amount of feed needed will vary depending on the size of the chicken, their age, and the climate. A good rule of thumb is to provide 1/4 to 1/3 pound of feed per chicken per day.

Q: Can I feed my chickens only scraps and kitchen waste?

A: No, chickens require a balanced diet that includes a source of protein, carbohydrates, and fats. While chickens can eat a variety of kitchen scraps, it's important to supplement their diet with a balanced feed that contains the proper nutrients.

Q: What are the best protein sources for chickens?

A: Good protein sources for chickens include soybeans, corn, peas, beans, and fish meal. It's also important to make sure that the protein source is non-genetically modified and free from pesticides and herbicides.

Q: How can I know if my chickens are getting enough nutrients from their feed?

A: You can know if your chickens are getting enough nutrients from their feed by observing their physical condition and behavior. Healthy chickens will have shiny feathers, bright eyes, and good weight. If you notice any problems, you may want to consult with a veterinarian or poultry nutritionist.

Q: How can I ensure that my homemade feed is nutritionally complete?

A: You can ensure that your homemade feed is nutritionally complete by following the balanced recipes that are included in this book. Always have a variety of ingredients, such as grains, legumes, and supplements. You can also consult with a veterinarian or poultry nutritionist for guidance.

Q: What are some common feeding problems that I may encounter when making my own feed?

A: Some common feeding problems include picky eaters, nutrient deficiencies, and digestive issues. These problems can often be resolved by adjusting the ingredients in your feed, or by providing additional supplements.

Q: Can I store homemade feed for long periods of time?

A: Homemade feed should be stored in a cool, dry place and used within a few months. Whole grains and seeds can be stored for longer periods, but once they are ground into a meal or mixed with other ingredients, they will lose their nutritional value over time.

Q: Is it necessary to add mineral supplements to my chickens' diet?

A: Chickens need a balance of minerals in their diet for optimal health. If your chickens have access to a variety of forage, they will likely get the minerals they need. However, if they are confined and eating a mostly grain-based diet, it's a good idea to supplement with minerals.

Conclusion

In conclusion, raising chickens can be a rewarding and fun experience, but it's important to provide them with the proper nutrition to keep them healthy and happy. By understanding the basics of chicken feed and learning to make your own feed, you can have more control over the quality of the food you provide for your birds. By following the information provided in this book, you can ensure that your chickens receive a balanced diet that will support their growth, egg production, and overall health. Remember to always consult with a veterinarian or other poultry expert if you have any concerns about your chickens' health or nutrition. With the right knowledge and care, your chickens will thrive and provide you with eggs and meat for years to come. Thank you for reading, and we hope that this book has been a valuable resource for you in your journey of raising chickens.

Happy farming!